Remembering
Huntsville

Jacquelyn Procter Reeves

TURNER
PUBLISHING COMPANY

In the center of South Side Square was the T. T. Terry Building. In huge letters across the top of the building was their slogan, "GREAT IS THE POWER OF CASH."

Remembering
Huntsville

Turner Publishing Company
www.turnerpublishing.com

Remembering Huntsville

Library of Congress Control Number: 2010924301

ISBN: 978-1-59652-647-1

Printed in the United States of America

ISBN: 978-1-68336-840-3 (pbk.)

CONTENTS

John Stallworth, third from left, is honored by his college alma mater, Alabama A & M University. John went on to become a pro football player (wide receiver) with the Pittsburgh Steelers before returning to Huntsville to become a successful businessman. After a stellar career, he was named to the NFL Hall of Fame. He still holds Super Bowl records.

ACKNOWLEDGMENTS

This volume, *Remembering Huntsville,* is the result of the cooperation and efforts of many individuals, organizations, and corporations. It is with great thanks that we acknowledge the valuable contribution of the Huntsville Public Library staff for their generous support.

We would also like to thank the following individuals for valuable contributions and assistance in making this work possible:

Tim Griffin, Historian
Thomas Hutchens, Heritage Room, Huntsville Public Library
Jim Maples, Historian and Editor
Mona Mitchell, Technical Processing, Huntsville Public Library
Raneé Pruitt, Archivist, Huntsville Public Library
Robert Reeves, who identified the dates of many photographs by the automobiles in them

---

This project represents countless hours of review and research. The researchers and writer have reviewed hundreds of photographs. We greatly appreciate the generous assistance of the archives listed here, without whom this project could not have been completed.

The goal in publishing the work is to provide broader access to a set of extraordinary photographs. The aim is to inspire, provide perspective, and evoke insight that might assist officials and citizens, who together are responsible for determining Huntsville's future. In addition, the book seeks to preserve the past with respect and reverence.

With the exception of touching up imperfections that have accrued with the passage of time and cropping where necessary, no changes have been made. The focus and clarity of many images are limited to the technology and the ability of the photographer at the time they were recorded.

We encourage readers to reflect as they explore Huntsville, stroll along its streets, or wander its neighborhoods. It is the publisher's hope that in making use of this work, longtime residents will learn something new and that new residents will gain a perspective on where Huntsville has been, so that each can contribute to its future.

—*Todd Bottorff, Publisher*

PREFACE

What is a photograph? More than ink on paper, a record of the past, or an image in time, a photograph captures a moment that can never be recreated, a moment forever recorded that sparks the imagination not only of those who lived it but of those not yet born when the shutter was clicked.

Look into these images of the past and see the muddy streets, feel the chill that comes with the winter snow, listen to the brass band of a 4th of July parade, and cheer for the success of the moon landing. Imagine the wariness of the Union soldiers who occupied a Rebel town, as well as the fear of the residents under that occupation. We read about the many events in our history, but words are not enough to describe the joyous smiles on youngsters or the lined and weathered faces of veterans who saw war so many years before. We are fortunate to see these captured moments in time.

No images exist from 1805, when pioneer John Hunt established his home at the Big Spring, a body of water under a bluff that has served as the heart of this ever-changing community for more than 200 years. The town of Hunt's Spring became Twickenham for a brief period, before being permanently named Huntsville in honor of its first white settler. The first Constitutional Convention was held here in 1819, making Huntsville the provisional capital as well as the county seat. Cotton thrived in the rich soil. It represented a source of wealth for some but back-breaking labor for the large number of slaves brought here to harvest the "white gold."

A few of these images may look familiar to Huntsvillians and former residents, but many are of places lost to the ravages of fire and urban renewal. Our structures of 150 years ago dictated taste and refinement, an ideal now overshadowed by cost and efficiency. Few of us can comprehend the hustle and bustle of our downtown in past decades, before television drew us inside and shopping malls pulled customers and stores to the suburbs. Many of these pictures from the past, never before published, are now available for the first time to new generations.

Many people helped create this book. Without their expertise and enthusiasm, we could not offer this treasure. We appreciate their willingness to share their knowledge.

Millions of photographs are taken every day—for a special occasion or no particular reason at all. In our distant past, however, very few pictures were made and even fewer have survived. Look at the faces of those long gone and feel their pride and their heartaches and imagine their everyday lives. Will future generations wonder about our own lives, long after we are gone, as they gaze into our eyes captured in photographs? Of course they will! Though buildings come and go, our images, and perhaps even a smidgen of our personalities, will remain in each and every timeless photograph.

—*Jacquelyn Procter Reeves*

Madison County's second courthouse was designed by architect George Steele. This beautiful Greek Revival structure was built in 1835 and torn down in 1914. The dome was copper-clad. A sign at the gate states, "Five dollar fine for hitching within ten feet of this gate."

WAR AND RECONSTRUCTION

(1860–1899)

Bringing cotton into town to sell was a big event for farmers and spectators, as seen in this 1860 photograph.

Two tents occupy the open lot on East Side Square, known as Cheap Side Row. Churches in the background are the Presbyterian Church, the old Episcopal Church, and the Church of the Nativity. There is speculation that the tents belonged to Union soldiers who occupied Huntsville during the Civil War. Barely visible in the upper left side of the picture is the partially obscured front of LeRoy Pope's mansion on Echols Hill. He was the grandfather of LeRoy Pope Walker, first secretary of war for the Confederate States of America.

Huntsville was captured by Union soldiers in April 1862 and occupied, off and on, throughout the war. This photograph shows the Union tent city erected around the courthouse.

This 1867 photograph of the South Side Square suggests a slow business day. Horses are tethered at the iron fence surrounding the courthouse. None of the original buildings constructed on this block now exist.

Wagons of cotton clogged the Courthouse Square while residents came to enjoy an eventful day in town.

East Side Square is bustling with activity after a heavy rain. What a sloppy mess!

A cow meanders down the street in front of the Presbyterian Church. This was the second Presbyterian Church on this site, finished and dedicated in 1860. It was said to have "the handsomest building, the tallest spire, the biggest bell, the finest organ, the four richest bronze chandeliers, and the highest-priced pews in the city." The spire was blown down by a storm in 1878.

This photograph, taken around 1880, is of Engine House No. 1 and the City Scales, located between Washington and Jefferson streets.

Completed in 1872, the magnificent City Hall building on the corner of Jefferson Street and Clinton Avenue burned down in 1911. This photograph was taken in 1882.

Thompson Land & Investment Co. specialized in buying and selling farm land in and around Huntsville. Their advertisement boasted they were "one of the most progressive and widely known Real Estate Companies in the South."

Six men and one youngster pose in front of the second Madison County Courthouse. The fence now borders the back of Maple Hill Cemetery.

A light dusting of snow didn't keep Huntsvillians away from downtown on a busy Saturday afternoon. This view is taken from the corner of Jefferson Street and North Side Square looking toward East Side Square.

A dam and city waterworks were built at the Big Spring. The bluff overlooking the spring is at the left.

This photograph, taken in the late 1800s, may be of a funeral. Legend says Union soldiers refused to stable their horses inside the Church of the Nativity Episcopal even though they were ordered to do so during the Civil War. The reason? Over the entrance of the chapel are the words, "Reverence My Sanctuary."

The Federal Courthouse, an imposing and impressive structure built on the corner of Eustis and Greene streets in 1890, was torn down in 1954.

E. C. Yarbrough, center, and Joe Yarbrough, right, stand in front of the E. C. Yarbrough Grocery and Feed Store in this 1890 photograph. It was located on the corner of Washington and Randolph streets.

Wages were low for mill workers. Unions stepped in to help improve working conditions, but mill owners usually responded by temporarily shutting down operations, throwing employees out of work while negotiations were going on.

The sign at the left says it all: "This is not the place for the first Quarrel." The young boy appears deep in thought as the man in front walks across a precarious plank with a bucket of water. Note the man sitting cross-legged on the bluff. Cold Spring was located on Monte Sano Mountain.

Dignitaries and workers pose while construction continues on the Monte Sano Railroad. The workers are holding heavy pick-axes.

The Monte Sano Hotel was built as a health resort, but traveling the primitive road in a Tally-ho coach was tedious. For easier access from the downtown Huntsville depot, a dummy-line railway was constructed. This 1890 photograph shows the impressive engineering design of its trestle. "Dummy line" in this case refers to a private rail line not maintained by the railroad company; in essence, a dead-end line.

A rock crusher at work on the Monte Sano Railway. Fliers advertised "For pleasure, convenience, safety and beautiful scenery, take the Monte Sano Standard Gauge Railway." Unfortunately, the railroad up to the resort was full of hairpin turns and frightened many tourists.

Built in 1892, the Dallas Cotton Mill was a huge employer. More than 1,000 workers operated 1,500 looms and 59,000 spindles. The Dallas Mill ceased operation in 1952, and the vacant building burned to the ground in a horrendous 1991 fire.

The Dallas Mill was the center of the mill village that grew up around it. Even children worked at the local mills under terrible conditions until Child Labor Laws came into effect in the twentieth century.

The gatekeeper lived in this house at the tollgate to Monte Sano Mountain. Note the richly upholstered horse carriage to the right. Present-day Tollgate Road retains the name of those long-ago days.

The I. Schiffman Store on the corner of Eustis Street and East Side Square was the 1902 birthplace of screen actress Tallulah Bankhead. It has changed little in appearance since the stone facade was added in 1895.

Southern Bell Telephone and Telegraph Company officially opened July 28, 1896, when Mayor W. T. Hutchens called the General Superintendent of Southern Bell in New York. The first long-distance words from Huntsville were, "The city of Huntsville, her people, send greetings to New York, hoping that the long distance telephone may be of both pleasure and profit to her people."

The new pump house at the Big Spring, completed in 1898.

Thousands of spindles operated simultaneously in the spinning room at the Merrimack Mill.

Barbers dressed in high style sport handlebar mustaches and cater to the needs of the uptown clientele. Note the stationary barber chairs.

A severe winter cold snap, rare this far South, leaves icicles at the Big Spring in 1899.

The fire station was attached to city hall, located on the corner of Washington Street and Clinton Avenue. Firemen and horses pose with their equipment in this photograph.

An Industrial Revolution

(1900–1919)

Dallas mill workers posed for this photograph. Note the boys, some as young as ten years old, who worked long hours for low pay. Child labor laws put children into schoolrooms instead of factories early in the twentieth century.

The contract to build the Lowe Cotton Mill was granted in 1900 to produce thread. Note the cotton patch in the common ground. The building on the right still stands in West Huntsville.

This photograph from around 1900 shows a stylishly dressed woman identified as "Mrs. Monroe" riding her carriage past the Federal Courthouse located on Greene Street. This impressive building was a casualty of urban renewal.

Two horses are gaudily dressed for the 1901 4th of July Parade. Inside the buggy are former Mayor Thomas Smith and Frank Murphy. Laughlin Funeral Home and Furniture Store stands behind them.

The sign at T. B. Overton's Washington Street establishment advertises horseshoeing as their speciality.
In addition to repairing farm equipment, they also sold crop fertilizer.

R. L. Sparkman, pictured on the right, carved many of the old headstones in local cemeteries. His business, Sparkman Marble & Granite, shared a building with the harness shop on East Side Square before it moved adjacent to Maple Hill Cemetery.

This photograph, taken in December 1904, shows one of Huntsville's smaller "flouring" mills, Spring City Mills, which was on West Clinton Street.

The Cumberland Presbyterian Church, first organized in the early 1800s, finally had a finished building in 1850. It was later torn down, a new building was erected over the same foundation, and it was dedicated at the time this photograph was taken. This building is now the Central Presbyterian Church.

Many people will remember shopping at the dry goods store on the corner of Clinton Avenue and Washington Street. The business was known by several names before it became Dunnavant's. The building was gutted by fire in 1941 but was soon rebuilt.

These distinguished gentlemen are members of the Oddfellows organization.

The dedication of a Confederate monument to honor the many young men from Huntsville who fought for the South during the Civil War was a well-attended event in November 1905.

Deserted streets with South Side Square on the right and the third courthouse on the left. The Confederate monument stands high above the brick streets, crisscrossed with streetcar tracks.

West Side Square, also known as Cotton Row, was busy during the cotton season. The bank known as "The Marble Palace" is seen at the far right and the monument to Confederate soldiers is at the left.

This photograph of the Merrimack Mills baseball team was taken about 1906. Joe Bradley, Sr., is standing at right and Superintendent Gordon Cobb stands to the left.

The Huntsville Hotel, built in 1858, burned to the ground in 1911 along with the annex, the opera house, and several businesses. This site, now occupied by a bank, is located on Jefferson Street near the Courthouse Square.

Several men, possibly employees, pose for a photograph inside London Plumbing Company at the corner of Clinton Avenue and Gallatin Street in 1907. Note the claw-foot bathtubs and ornate stove.

Members of a Baptist church Sunday school posed for this picture about 1909. Billie Buckner, Merrimack Mill's first gatekeeper, is the man with the long beard at the right.

Three people dressed for an outing pose on their horses. Note the curious look on the horse at left.

Members of the junior class at Huntsville High School dressed in their best clothes for this 1914 picture.

The axes and emblems suggest these men may have been members of Woodmen of the World, founded in 1890 as a benevolent fraternal organization.

A streetcar ambles past a horse-drawn buggy on Clinton Avenue while Central Café prepares to feed hungry customers.

The Benevolent & Protective Order of Elks (BPOE) Lodge Number 698 entered this elaborately decorated car in a local parade. Note their "hood ornament."

This photograph was taken in the Probate Office of the second Madison County Courthouse.

Members of the fire department pose in March 1919. It was a sad day for the fire house horses when they were put to pasture.

The third Madison County Courthouse, constructed in 1913, had an old-time clock tower. The building was replaced by the present modern high-rise in the 1960s.

This postcard, looking south on Jefferson Street, captured Huntsville's bustling scene. Traffic lights had become a necessity. The Grand Theater is on the left.

During the 1920s, the fire department and city hall were located on Madison Street. Brass was polished and cars shined for this photograph.

Prosperity to the Great Depression

(1920–1939)

Traffic lights, like this one at the corner of Greene Street and Clinton Avenue, were once turned on with a key by local police officers. This picture was taken in 1924.

The 4th of July Parade brought everyone out to celebrate in style. This family sedan was transformed into an impressive float.

A local office supply company carried all the latest office needs.

Saint Mary's Church of the Visitation was organized in 1861. The Civil War interrupted construction, which was not finished until 1872. Father Jeremiah Trecy was one of several local clergymen arrested by Federal troops during the war.

These happy people are teachers from Joe Bradley School, taking a picnic break in 1925.

The American Legion held a convention in Huntsville in 1927. Local resident George Mahoney sits on the running board of a limousine.

Clark Steadman's Bar B Q was a popular eatery, featuring the local favorite—barbecue. A pinball machine beckons a man with loose change on the left. Clark Steadman stands second from right.

A vendor's stand sits on the Clinton Avenue side of the corner of Washington Street and Clinton Avenue. The building behind it has undergone renovation, but still resembles its 1930s appearance.

Members of Huntsville High School's football team pose in this 1930 photograph with their coach, Jesse Keene, who wears a Vanderbilt shirt in the third row.

This 1932 Washington Street scene looking south shows thriving businesses despite the Great Depression sweeping the nation.

Members of the Madison County Sheriff's office stand in front of the city jail built on Washington Street in 1930. Sheriff Frank G. Hereford, who served from 1911–1915 and again from 1935–1937, is standing fourth from the left.

The congregation of this church formed in 1929 and built their church on East Clinton Street. Their first service here was held in 1937. Although the original building still stands, the size of the church has expanded considerably.

Shoppers walk along Washington Street in this photograph facing south.

Civil War veterans and two former slaves who went with their masters into war pose in 1938 in front of the marker dedicated by the Twickenham Chapter Daughters of the American Revolution. It was at this spot, on the corner of Gates and Franklin Streets, where 44 delegates met in 1819 to draft Alabama's constitution. This block is now Alabama's Constitution Village, a museum complex which recreates the buildings that stood here in 1819.

The Temple B'nai Sholom was founded in 1876. This Romanesque-Renaissance Revival building was dedicated in 1899. It remains the oldest synagogue in continuous use in the State of Alabama.

Monte Sano Park was dedicated on August 25, 1938. Dignitaries included Senator John Sparkman and Congressman William Bankhead, father of actress Talullah Bankhead. Bankhead National Forest in Northwest Alabama was named in his honor.

Dancers cut a rug to Big Band music at Dallas Street Armory.

FROM COTTON FIELDS TO ROCKET SHIPS

(1940–1970s)

Charming ladies sit on floats rounding the corner at Courthouse Square during a 1939 parade.

Building 7101 served as the first headquarters for Redstone Arsenal. It was built in 1941. A Hermes Missile is on display at the right.

Mill workers at Huntsville Manufacturing Company check spools to keep them humming.

A parade was held to celebrate Army Day on April 6, 1942. The Redstone Ordnance Plant sent several vehicles to participate. The Ordnance Plant was renamed Redstone Arsenal on February 26, 1943.

Backwoods trails all across Monte Sano Mountain made it a great place for horseback riding.

A group of ladies saddle up at a dude ranch on Monte Sano Mountain.

Confederate veterans gather for a reunion. J. A. Steger, the bespectacled man sitting just to the left of the man holding the Confederate flag, died at age 102 in 1948. He was the last living Civil War veteran from Madison County.

The eloquent Henderson National Bank, located to the right and on the corner of Randolph and Washington Streets, burned in 1946.

These people lined up around the block may have been waiting to apply for jobs or sign up for unemployment benefits. A Chapman Dairy truck sits on the right side of the street.

Even the children display their patriotism during a World War II–era parade.

The annual Cotton Ball was a big celebration, even if you didn't know the difference between a cotton boll or a boll weevil!

The Russel Erskine Hotel towers in the background at the left. It was named for Huntsville native Albert Russel Erskine, who became the millionaire president of Studebaker Automobile in South Bend, Indiana. He took his own life after the company went into receivership in 1933.

F. W. Woolworth Company on Washington Street was the original "5 and Dime" store. The sign to the far right at Kress' Store reveals inflation: "5-10-25."

Southern Furniture Store opened in 1946. Ten years later, local disc jockey Grady Reeves sat in the display window to promote the Trade-O-Rama. Anyone who caught him sleeping during the 67-hour marathon would win a new range or refrigerator.

This photograph of the office at Dallas Manufacturing Company was taken in March 1948.

"Bumper Lite" tape was placed on this city sedan as part of a Junior Chamber (J. C.) campaign to promote automobile safety in 1953.

Workers at Huntsville Manufacturing strike for higher wages in 1951, a common scene at many local mills and businesses.

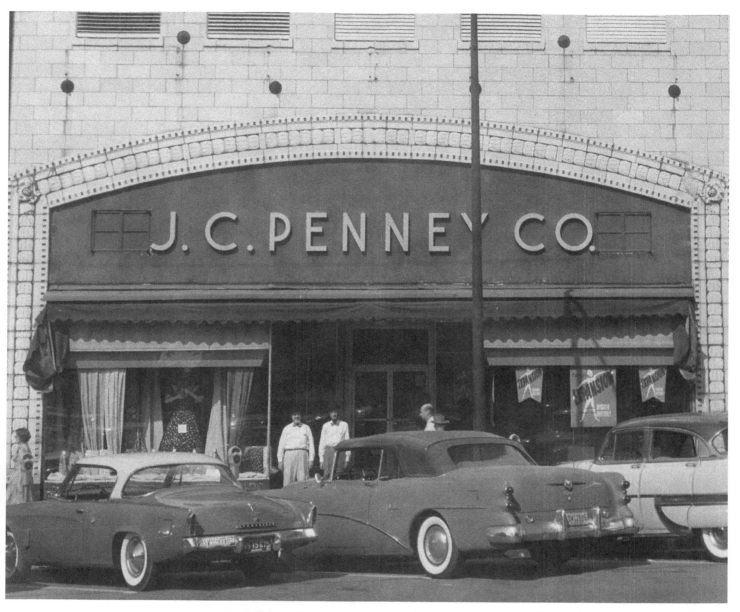

J. C. Penney Company promised stylish clothing at reasonable prices. A 1953 Studebaker Loewy Coup is parked in front. Like most retail stores, J. C. Penney moved to the mall in 1966. This building, on East Side Square, is now a law library.

The Big Spring Pool was a popular place for kids and adults to escape the summer heat, but like many facilities of the time, it was only open to whites. Boys in the water make faces and wave to the photographer.

This chain-link fence was placed around the Big Spring to deter anyone from sabotaging the water supply during World War II but remained in place for several years after the war.

This photograph of the office of Standard Loan Company, located at 112 ½ North Washington Street, was taken on December 20, 1954. Employees were working late that night, according to the wall clock.

This historic photograph is of the German "Paper Clip" Scientists and their wives taking the oath to become American Citizens in 1954. Recruited from postwar Europe under Operation Paperclip, a Cold War program to obtain German rocket scientists for the U.S. and deny them to the Soviet Union, many chose to turn their initial six-month stay into a lifetime in their new country.

A Christmas float sponsored by the *Huntsville Times* features "elves" who seem a little apprehensive in this parade around 1955. Santa sits in his sleigh and tosses candy to the children in the crowd. In the background is Hill's, which burned in 1962, and two cafes that were torn down in the 1970s.

An event at the Courthouse Square shows a number of booths set up all around the park. Sailors pose with pretty young ladies, near the U.S. Naval Reserve booth to the right. This photo was taken on May 21, 1955, by a U.S. Navy photographer.

Good weather invited people outside to mingle at the Courthouse Square. Before television drew people inside, downtown Huntsville was rarely deserted. Members of the U.S. Naval Reserve have a booth to show off their work and maybe even recruit a few new members.

A parade to celebrate Huntsville's Sesquicentennial gave civilians a chance to cheer for members of the armed forces in September 1955. The photographer was facing North Side Square,

North Side Square is unusually quiet, an indication that this is probably a Sunday or holiday. Sno-Wite Hamburgers cost 12 cents. Next door was Arnold's, a record shop owned by Arnold Hornbuckle. The steeple of the Methodist Church rises at the far right.

The V-2 Missile, developed by Germans in World War II, was studied by American scientists when von Braun and his team of rocket scientists came to America. This missile "as used for high altitude research firings at White Sands" was on display at the Courthouse Square.

The opening of Parkway Center, a modern strip mall, was a cause to celebrate on March 14, 1957.

Spectators admire Navy men in summer "Cracker Jacks" uniforms during a patriotic parade in 1956.

A banner on the back of the American Legion's mock locomotive in 1957 reflects the pride of these Huntsville residents.

With the exception of the I. Schiffman building on the right, all other businesses on East Side Square have changed. Today, most are attorneys' offices and the Law Library.

A car accident, involving a 1958 Chevrolet cab, brings the fire department out as water gushes from the hydrant. The Ritz Café was a popular place for local businessmen to have lunch. See the partial face of a boy peeking out from behind the street sign.

Jimmy Walker, Mayor R. B. Searcy, Stuart Jones, and Dorsey Uptain "launch" a symbolic rocket to celebrate the successful launching of the Explorer I Satellite in January, 1958.

A nighttime celebration was held on March 5, 1959, to commemorate the success of the Pioneer IV Moon Probe. The Space Age made Huntsville the Rocket Capital of the World.

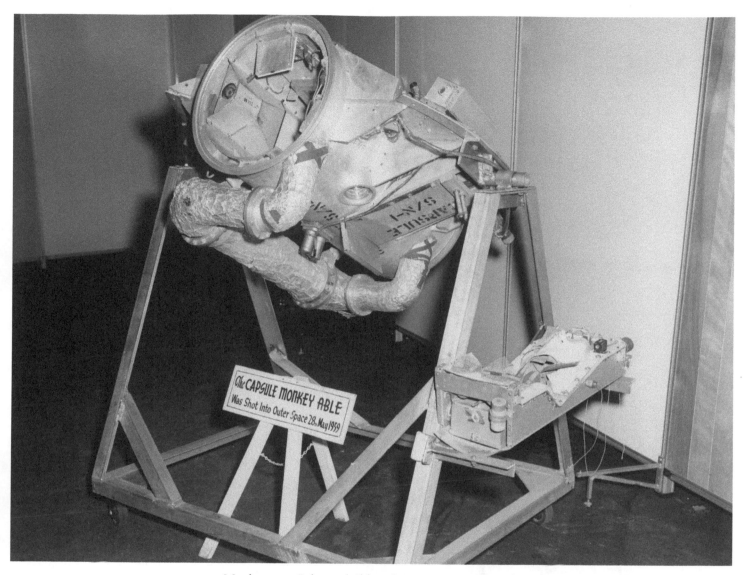

Monkeynauts Baker and Able rode into space on May 28, 1959. They survived the flight, but Able died on June 5 as technicians removed recording devices. Miss Baker lived for more than two decades after that historic flight.

Miss Baker, the celebrity monkey, enjoyed her retirement at the U.S. Space and Rocket Center, where she is now buried.

THE ORIGINAL
von BRAUN TEAM
CAME TO HUNTSVILLE
IN 1950

A few members of Dr. von Braun's team are gathered for a public event in 1959.

Wernher von Braun addressed a crowd gathered at the Courthouse Square to commemorate Astronaut Alan B. Shepard's 302-mile ride into space aboard the Redstone Rocket at a speed of 5,100 miles per hour. Huntsville was proud to boast that the rocket was designed and built locally. In addition, the mission was managed at Marshall Space Flight Center.

Park benches in front of the courthouse seem to be a natural place to sit and people-watch in this 1964 photo. Across the street, the Amusement Parlor offered billiards, next to Kennamer's Mill Ends Store. Posters on the fence announce Century 21 Shows will be in town September 28 to October 3.

This scene of South Side Square in 1965 reflects the change of businesses in downtown Huntsville as family stores were moving to strip malls and closer to Memorial Parkway and University Drive.

An aerial view of the east side of Washington Street looking north shows the Huntsville Times Building in the far background in this 1966 photograph.

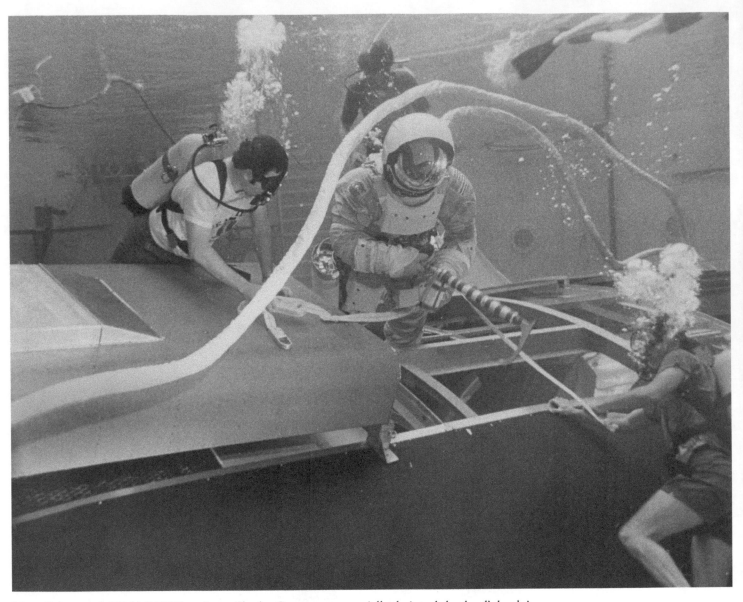

Navy divers watch NASA/MSFC engineer Charles Cooper use a specially designed shepherd's hook in the Neutral Buoyancy Simulator.

A miniature satellite hangs suspended from a globe above a model of the moon's surface. This 1968 photograph was taken at NASA.

General Charles W. Eifler, 3rd from right, signed this photograph of local dignitaries. General Eifler served three tours of duty at Redstone Arsenal: Commandant of United States Army Ordnance Guided Missile School, Deputy Commanding General Lead Combat Systems for MICOM, and finally MICOM Commanding General. At the time of his death in Huntsville on September 20, 2005, he was the highest-ranking retired army general in the state. He is buried at Arlington National Cemetery.

July 24, 1969, was a historic day for the entire world. Apollo 11 astronauts returned safely to earth after their lunar landing and walk on the moon. Wernher von Braun, the leader of America's race to space, was carried on the shoulders of proud Huntsville residents as the citizens of the city rushed to the courthouse to celebrate.

A balloon being inflated with helium at Redstone Arsenal, September 10, 1971.

Alabama's Governor George Wallace makes a stop in Huntsville with his wife Cornelia in June 1971.

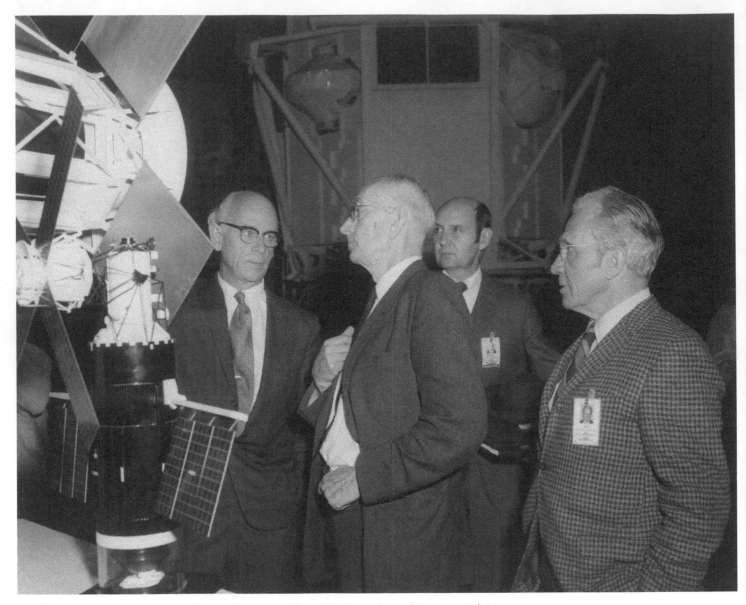

Dr. Ernst Stuhlinger; Dr. Brian O'Brien, Chairman of NASA's Space Council Program Advisory Council; Dr. George Bucher; and Dr. Harvey Hall inspect a model of the Skylab in 1971. Dr. O'Brien was given a briefing on the Marshall Space Flight Center's work on the space shuttle, space station, and future space flights.

The hit Broadway musical *Irene* dazzled Huntsvillians at Von Braun Civic Center Concert Hall in February 1976.

Cotton remained the staple of local farmers more than a century and a half after Huntsville was first settled. These bales are stacked near the Dallas Mill warehouse to be graded and weighed.

Legendary Alabama football coach Paul "Bear" Bryant carries his trademark hat as he walks a downtown street on "Honor America Day." County Commissioner James Record is at the extreme left. Huntsville's current mayor, Loretta Spencer, holds Bryant's arm.

Notes on the Photographs

These notes, listed by page number, attempt to include all aspects known of the photographs. Each of the photographs is identified by the page number, a title or description, photographer and collection, archive, and call or box number when applicable. Although every attempt was made to collect all data, in some cases complete data may have been unavailable due to the age and condition of some of the photographs and records.

II **SOUTH SIDE SQUARE**
Huntsville Public Library

VI **JOHN STALLWORTH**
Huntsville Public Library

X **COURTHOUSE**
Huntsville Public Library

2 **BRINGING IN COTTON**
Huntsville Public Library

3 **EAST SIDE SQUARE**
Huntsville Public Library

4 **UNION TENT CITY**
Huntsville Public Library

5 **SOUTH SIDE SQUARE**
Huntsville Public Library

6 **WAGONS OF COTTON**
Huntsville Public Library

7 **EAST SIDE SQUARE**
Huntsville Public Library

8 **PRESBYTERIAN CHURCH**
Huntsville Public Library

9 **ENGINE HOUSE NO. 1**
Huntsville Public Library

10 **CITY HALL**
Huntsville Public Library

11 **THOMPSON LAND & INVESTMENT**
Huntsville Public Library

12 **MADISON COUNTY COURTHOUSE**
Huntsville Public Library

13 **JEFFERSON STREET**
Huntsville Public Library

14 **CITY WATERWORKS**
Huntsville Public Library

15 **CHURCH OF NATIVITY**
Huntsville Public Library

16 **FEDERAL COURTHOUSE**
Huntsville Public Library

17 **GROCERY STORE**
Huntsville Public Library

18 **MILL WORKERS**
Huntsville Public Library

19 **COLD SPRING**
Huntsville Public Library

20 **RAILROAD WORKERS**
Huntsville Public Library

21 **DUMMY-LINE RAILWAY**
Huntsville Public Library

22 **ROCK CRUSHER**
Huntsville Public Library

23 **DALLAS COTTON MILL**
Huntsville Public Library

24 **DALLAS MILL**
Huntsville Public Library

25 **GATEKEEPER'S HOUSE**
Huntsville Public Library

26 **SCHIFFMAN STORE**
Huntsville Public Library

27 **SOUTHERN BELL**
Huntsville Public Library

28 **PUMP HOUSE**
Huntsville Public Library

29 **MERRIMACK MILL**
Huntsville Public Library

30 **BARBERS' HIGH STYLE**
Huntsville Public Library

31 **ICE AT BIG SPRING**
Huntsville Public Library

32 **FIRE DEPARTMENT**
Huntsville Public Library

34 **MILL WORKERS**
Huntsville Public Library

35 **LOWE MILL**
Huntsville Public Library

36 **WOMAN IN CARRIAGE**
Huntsville Public Library

37 **HORSES PULLING CARRIAGE**
Huntsville Public Library

Printed in the USA
CPSIA information can be obtained
at www.ICGtesting.com
JSHW072024140824
68134JS00042B/3776